THE ULTIMATE ANIMAL LIBRARY

Sea Horses

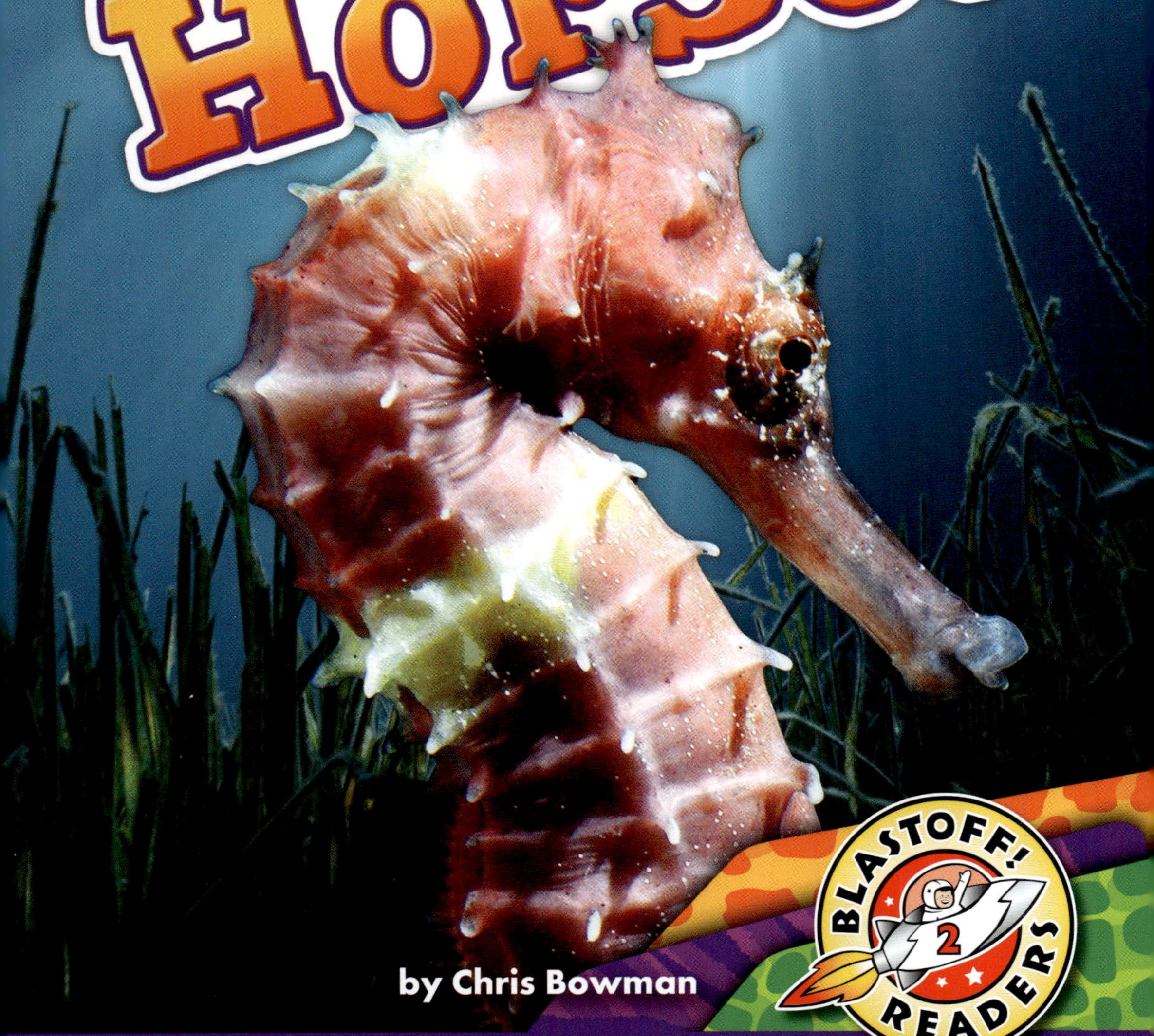

by Chris Bowman

BLASTOFF! READERS 2

BELLWETHER MEDIA • MINNEAPOLIS, MN

Blastoff! Readers are carefully developed by literacy experts to build reading stamina and move students toward fluency by combining standards-based content with developmentally appropriate text.

Level 1 provides the most support through repetition of high-frequency words, light text, predictable sentence patterns, and strong visual support.

Level 2 offers early readers a bit more challenge through varied sentences, increased text load, and text-supportive special features.

Level 3 advances early-fluent readers toward fluency through increased text load, less reliance on photos, advancing concepts, longer sentences, and more complex special features.

★ **Blastoff! Universe**

This edition first published in 2025 by Bellwether Media, Inc.

Library of Congress Cataloging-in-Publication Data

Names: Bowman, Chris, 1990- author.
Title: Sea horses / by Chris Bowman.
Description: Minneapolis, MN : Bellwether Media, Inc., 2025. | Series: Blastoff! Readers: The Ultimate Animal Library | Includes bibliographical references and index. | Audience: Ages 5-8 | Audience: Grades 2-3 | Summary: "Relevant images match informative text in this introduction to sea horses. Intended for students in kindergarten through third grade"-- Provided by publisher.
Identifiers: LCCN 2024038368 (print) | LCCN 2024038369 (ebook) | ISBN 9798893042450 (library binding) | ISBN 9798893043426 (ebook)
Subjects: LCSH: Sea horses--Juvenile literature.
Classification: LCC QL638.S9 B684 2025 (print) | LCC QL638.S9 (ebook) | DDC 597/.6798--dc23/eng/20240927
LC record available at https://lccn.loc.gov/2024038368
LC ebook record available at https://lccn.loc.gov/2024038369

Editor: Elizabeth Neuenfeldt Series Designer: Veah Demmin

Printed in the United States of America, North Mankato, MN.

Table of Contents

What Are Sea Horses? 4
Tiny Hiders 12
Growing Up 18
Glossary 22
To Learn More 23
Index 24

What Are Sea Horses?

Sea horses are fish. They live in waters around the world. Sea horses have long **snouts**. Their heads look like horse heads!

Patagonian Sea Horse Report

Range

Status in the Wild

Habitats

Some sea horses are as small as 0.5 inches (1.3 centimeters) long.

Others are as big as 14 inches (35.6 centimeters) long!

Sea horses have long, curled tails that hold onto plants. **Currents** cannot carry them away.

Their bodies are covered with bony plates.

Sea horses swim upright. Fins help them move forward and turn.

Their **swim bladders** move them up and down.

Spot a Sea Horse

Tiny Hiders

Sea horses live alone in warm, **shallow** waters. Some live on **coral reefs**.

Others live in seagrasses or in **mangrove forests**.

Most sea horses live in **territories**. Males stay in smaller areas than females.

male sea horse

Sea horses hold on to coral or seagrass with their tails.

Sea horses hide well amongst plants. It helps them catch **prey**. They suck in shrimp and **plankton**.

They also stay safe from **predators**.

Growing Up

Female sea horses lay up to 2,000 eggs in males' **brood pouches**.

Male sea horses carry the eggs until they **hatch**. Then they give birth to **fry**!

brood
pouch

Sea horse fry live on
their own right away.

Currents often carry them to a new home. Time for a new territory!

Life of a Sea Horse

Name of Babies

fry

Number of Eggs

up to 2,000

Time Spent in Eggs

around 2 to 4 weeks

Life Span

up to 5 years

Glossary

brood pouches—pockets on male sea horses' bodies that hold eggs

coral reefs—groups of corals that grow in warm, shallow ocean waters

currents—patterns of water movement in a body of water

fry—baby sea horses

hatch—to break open

mangrove forests—thick, tropical forests that can grow along coasts in salty swamp water

plankton—ocean plants or animals that drift in water; most plankton are tiny.

predators—animals that hunt other animals for food

prey—animals that are hunted by other animals for food

shallow—not deep

snouts—the noses and mouths of some animals

swim bladders—organs that help sea horses float in the water

territories—areas where animals live

To Learn More

AT THE LIBRARY

Moening, Kate. *Sea Horses.* Minneapolis, Minn.: Bellwether Media, 2022.

Neuenfeldt, Elizabeth. *Sea Horse.* Minneapolis, Minn.: Bellwether Media, 2021.

Sabelko, Rebecca. *Ocean Animals.* Minneapolis, Minn.: Bellwether Media, 2023.

ON THE WEB

FACTSURFER

Factsurfer.com gives you a safe, fun way to find more information.

1. Go to www.factsurfer.com.
2. Enter "sea horses" into the search box and click 🔍.
3. Select your book cover to see a list of related content.

Index

bodies, 9
bony plates, 9
brood pouches, 18, 19
coral, 15
coral reefs, 12
currents, 8, 21
eggs, 18
females, 14, 18
fins, 10
fish, 4
food, 16, 17
fry, 18, 20, 21
hatch, 18
heads, 4
hide, 16
life of a sea horse, 21
males, 14, 18
mangrove forests, 13
plants, 8, 13, 15, 16
predators, 17
prey, 16
range, 4, 5
size, 4, 6, 7, 8
snouts, 4
spot a sea horse, 11
status, 5
swim, 10
swim bladders, 10
tails, 8, 15
territories, 14, 21
waters, 4, 12

The images in this book are reproduced through the courtesy of: bluehand, front cover; Damsea, front cover background, interior background; Olkita, front cover (sea horse icon); Rich Carey, pp. 3, 14; Dennis van de Water, p. 4; kaschibo, p. 6; James Peake/ Alamy, p. 7; Basicdog, p. 8; Vladimir Wrangel, p. 9; Marcos del Mazo, p. 10; Kjeld Friis, pp. 10-11; boommaval, p. 11; GOLFX, p. 12; Vladislav Gajic, p. 13; Adam Leaders, p. 15; Thomas Aijian, pp. 16-17; Gazi Mahmud Al Maruf, p. 17 (crabs); Lorna Roberts, p. 17 (larger fish); Fotopogledi, p. 17 (sea horse); slowmotiongli, p. 17 (shrimp); Morgan Trimble/ Alamy, p. 17 (plankton); Rebecca Schreiner, p. 18; Nature Picture Library/ Alamy, pp. 18-19; S.Rohrlach, p. 20; Underwater/ Alamy, p. 21; Arunee Rodloy, p. 23.